Money Maketh Man

Money Habits, Investing, Saving, Spending, and Financial Lessons Many Learn Too Late

Picture a small apartment, mismatched furniture, and a fridge that echoes back with emptiness. Yeah, that was my life during the 'lean' years. Money was tighter than a pair of skinny jeans. But you know what? Those were some of the foundational and interesting moments of my life.

Living on a shoestring budget meant getting creative. Ramen noodles became a gourmet feast, and thrift store shopping was my version of high fashion. I learned to appreciate the simple joys—those cheap movie nights at home, the joy of finding a $5 bill in a forgotten pair of jeans, and the art of turning leftovers into culinary masterpieces.

But as life has a funny way of throwing curveballs, I found myself inching towards the 'average' lane. A steady job, a reliable income, and the luxury of not having to check my bank account before swiping my card. Suddenly, the world seemed a bit brighter, and the options a tad bit broader.

The 'average' stage had its perks, no doubt. Weekend getaways and dining at restaurants where the menu didn't have pictures were no longer reserved for the elite. Yet, it wasn't all rainbows and unicorns. There was a subtle pressure to keep up with the Joneses—or in today's terms, the Kardashians. The latest gadgets, the trendiest clothes, and the constant stream of social media flaunting made it easy to forget the simplicity that once brought so much joy.

It's during this phase that I realized the importance of financial literacy. It's not just about making money; it's about making smart decisions with it. Investments, savings, and the dreaded budgeting—all suddenly became part of my adulting arsenal. There's nothing like the thrill of seeing your savings account grow, or the satisfaction of making informed investment choices. It's like playing a strategic game, and guess what? You're the main player.

Now, let's fast forward to the 'rich' part of the saga. Ah, the land of milk and honey—or so they say. But here's the reality check: being rich doesn't mean endless extravagance and carefree spending. It's more like having a backstage pass to the concert of life—you get a better view, but you still need to decide which bands are worth listening to.

Yes, there are perks. Traveling without a budget, having the freedom to explore passions without worrying about bills, and the peace of mind that comes with financial security. But here's the twist—most wealthy people discover that the true richness lies in experiences, not possessions.

During the wealthier times, many embark on adventures that transcend the material realm. Volunteering in communities, supporting causes close to their hearts, and mentoring others in their financial journeys become their new luxuries. The fulfillment derived from giving back eclipses the fleeting joy of acquiring more stuff.

Oh, and let's not forget the importance of maintaining a grounded circle. True wealth isn't just measured in dollars but in the relationships you build. I've seen firsthand how money can alter people's perceptions, and I've learned to treasure those who stick around, whether I'm eating ramen or caviar.

It's not about reaching the end of the track but learning to enjoy every twist and turn. Each financial phase has its lessons—

poverty teaches resilience, the middle ground teaches balance, and affluence teaches responsibility.

"Enough"

You're strolling through a mall, minding your own business, and suddenly, the hypnotic glow of a storefront lures you in. There it is—the latest, shiniest, must-have gadget that promises to change your life. Your heart races, palms get a bit sweaty, and you start plotting the fastest route to the ATM. But hold up! What if, just for a moment, you paused and asked yourself, "Do I really need this, or is it just another blip on the 'wants' radar?"

It's not about denying yourself the pleasures of life; it's about discerning between genuine needs and the siren call of consumerism. We're bombarded daily with messages that scream, "You need this to be happy!" But what if, just what if, happiness wasn't in the next shiny thing but in acknowledging that what you have is, well, enough? We're told that satisfaction lies just around the corner, but spoiler alert: that corner doesn't exist. We're living in a world that glorifies excess, leaving us in a constant state of dissatisfaction. So, what's the antidote to this insatiable desire for more? The concept of "enough." It's a radical shift from the societal norm, an invitation to hit the pause button and take stock of what truly matters. How many times have you told yourself, "Once I earn X amount, then I'll be happy"? The finish line keeps moving, doesn't it?

When we embrace the concept of "enough," suddenly our possessions become intentional. We're not mindlessly accumulating; we're consciously choosing what adds value to our lives. It's a shift from the pursuit of possessions for their own sake to a mindful curation of a life rich in experiences and meaningful connections.

What if, instead of chasing every opportunity, we learned to say no to what doesn't align with our values and priorities? The joy of missing out is about cultivating a life that resonates with our authentic selves, free from the shackles of comparison and the pressure to conform. What if we embraced the messy, imperfect journey of pursuing our dreams, finding joy in the process rather than fixating on flawless outcomes?

"Financial Minimalism"

It's all too easy to find ourselves entangled in a web of financial commitments, subscriptions, and accounts, each demanding its own slice of attention and resources. The world bombards us with the message that more is better, that accumulation equates to success. But what if the path to true prosperity lay not in the abundance of possessions but in the intentional curation of a simpler, more focused financial life? This is the essence of financial minimalism - a call to simplicity that transcends the conventional narrative of wealth. To provide better context, distinguishing between essential and non-essential expenses was a very important step in my personal growth. Essential expenses were those directly contributing to my well-being and financial goals. Non-essential expenses, however, were like unnecessary baggage, weighing me down. It was time to discern which subscriptions and accounts were truly adding value to my life. I mean, We've all fallen prey to the Impulse Monster at some point. It lurks in the shadows of the checkout aisle, whispering sweet nothings about the irresistibility of that candy bar or the "buy one, get one free" deal on items we never knew we needed.

Every conscious spender needs a Spending Manifesto - a set of principles that guide financial choices. Craft your manifesto with care, articulating the values and aspirations that matter most to you. This becomes your compass in the tumultuous sea of consumerist temptations. The first step is to identify your non-negotiables - the aspects of life that you're unwilling to compromise on. Whether it's investing in personal development, supporting local businesses, or contributing to environmental sustainability, these become the pillars of your conscious spending philosophy. Just as minimalism advocates for decluttering physical spaces, conscious spending encourages a decluttering of financial habits. Conduct a financial detox, examining recurring expenses and subscriptions that no longer align with your values. Release the unnecessary to make room for the extraordinary. Letting go is an art, and it applies not only to possessions but also to financial habits that no longer serve you.

Financial minimalism isn't about living on the edge; it's about creating a safety net. Establishing an emergency fund became a cornerstone of my financial strategy, providing a buffer against unexpected expenses and offering peace of mind in turbulent times.

"10, 9, 8, 7, 6, 5, 4, 3, 2, 1, 0.

Don't buy!"

In the frenetic rhythm of modern life, where one-click purchases and impulsive spending temptations abound, there exists a simple yet transformative tool— the 10-Second Rule. Imagine this: before succumbing to the allure of that shiny new gadget or the irresistible flash sale, you grant yourself a mere 10 seconds—a brief pause that can redefine your relationship with money. The 10-Second Rule is not a complex financial theory devised by Wall Street wizards. It's a simple concept rooted in the understanding that impulsive decisions often lead to regret. By implementing a brief 10-second pause before making a purchase, you give yourself the time to assess whether the item is necessary, or just the excitement hormones controlling your nerves.

This rule taps into the science of decision-making. Our brains are wired to seek immediate rewards, often at the expense of long-term goals. The 10-Second Rule intervenes in this process, providing a moment for the more reflective, strategic part of our brain to weigh in. It's a pause that disrupts the autopilot mode of impulsive spending. It's also a countercultural act that challenges the notion that quick decisions equate to smart decisions. Whether it's the limited-time offer that screams urgency or the 'buy now, pay later' allure, the path to impulsive spending is riddled with enticements that prey on our desire for immediate satisfaction.

The allure of impulse buying lies in the ephemeral high it provides. It's the instant gratification of acquiring something new and exciting. However, this high is fleeting, leaving behind a residue of regret when the credit card statement arrives.

The first step in implementing the 10-Second Rule is to recognize the temptation. It could be the flashy display in a store, a persuasive online ad, or even the seemingly innocent shopping cart icon on your favorite e-commerce app. As you feel the gravitational pull towards the purchase, hit the pause button. Give yourself the gift of 10 seconds. It's a brief interlude that separates the impulse from the decision, allowing you to step back from the brink of immediate gratification.

In those 10 seconds, ask yourself a series of critical questions:

- Does this purchase satisfy an important need either long term or short term?
- Can I walk away from making this purchase and be very comfortable doing so?
- Can I afford this without compromising other financial priorities?

Could the funds be better allocated towards a more meaningful goal? Armed with insights from your 10-second reflection, make an informed choice. If the purchase aligns with your financial goals and brings genuine value, proceed with confidence. If not, gracefully step away, knowing that you've just thwarted a potential financial misstep.

"Save now, Party Later"

One of the most famous studies on delayed gratification is the Marshmallow Experiment conducted by psychologist Walter Mischel in the 1960s. Children were given a choice: eat one marshmallow immediately or wait for 15 minutes and receive two marshmallows. The study revealed that those who resisted the temptation for immediate gratification tended to have better life outcomes in areas like academic achievement and health.

Delayed gratification is a time-tested principle that extends beyond childhood experiments. It's the ability to resist immediate rewards in favor of more substantial benefits down the road. Psychologists describe the struggle between immediate and delayed gratification as a battle between two systems in the brain. System 1 is impulsive and seeks instant rewards, while

System 2 is more reflective and considers long-term consequences. Delayed gratification requires engaging System 2, training the mind to think beyond the immediate pleasure.

Owning a home is a significant financial goal for many. Rather than succumbing to the allure of a quick and easy mortgage approval, you decide to practice delayed gratification. You diligently save for a substantial down payment, ensuring better loan terms and long-term financial stability. The patience invested in the process transforms the home purchase into a well-earned achievement.

One of the primary challenges in practicing delayed gratification is the Fear of Missing Out (FOMO). Peer pressure can be a significant hurdle in the path of delayed gratification. The desire to keep up with friends or colleagues who indulge in lavish spending may create internal conflicts. Building a strong sense of self-awareness and the ability to stay true to your financial values helps in circumnavigating peer pressure without compromising your commitment to delayed gratification.

"Congratulations! You are $1 richer"

One of the beauties of the reverse punishment system is that it allows you to celebrate even the smallest financial victories. Did you manage to resist that impulse purchase? Reward yourself! Did you save a little extra money this month? Treat yourself! By acknowledging and celebrating these small wins, you reinforce positive financial behaviors.

The rewards you choose play a crucial role in the success of the reverse punishment system. These rewards should be meaningful to you, serving as a motivating factor for achieving your financial goals. Whether it's a special treat, a day off, or a small splurge, the reward should make you feel good about your accomplishments.

Now, let's talk about creating a structured reward system. Assign specific rewards to different financial milestones. For example, if you successfully stick to your budget for a month, treat yourself to a nice dinner. If you consistently save a certain percentage of your income, plan a weekend getaway. The key is to make the rewards proportionate to the effort and achievement.

Positive reinforcement isn't just about rewarding specific goals; it's about building positive money habits over time. As you consistently meet your financial goals and receive rewards, these positive behaviors become ingrained in your lifestyle. It's a gradual process that transforms the way you approach money management.

Dopamine, often referred to as the "feel-good" neurotransmitter, plays a significant role in positive reinforcement. When you achieve a financial goal and receive a reward, your brain releases dopamine, creating a sense of pleasure and satisfaction. This neurochemical response strengthens the connection between the behavior (meeting financial goals) and the reward, making you more inclined to repeat the positive behavior.

Instead of viewing financial management as a burdensome task, you start associating it with achievements, growth, and self-improvement. This shift in mindset is a game-changer when it comes to long-term financial well-being. Implementing a reverse punishment system is not without its challenges. It requires discipline, consistency, and a commitment to changing old habits. However, by focusing on positive reinforcement, you can turn these challenges into opportunities for growth. Each hurdle becomes a chance to learn and refine your approach to financial management. Instead of focusing solely on the "don'ts" and restrictions, emphasize the "dos" and the rewards that come with responsible financial behavior. This approach can be particularly effective in educating children and young adults about the importance of managing money wisely.

"I Don't want to be a homeless Bum!"

We've all had those moments when we look at our bank statements or credit card bills and think, "I don't want to end up like that." It's a natural response to financial stress, and it's time to harness that fear in a constructive way. Anti-goals, in personal finance, involve identifying the pitfalls and financial missteps we want to avoid at all costs. Take a moment to reflect on your financial fears. What scenarios make you cringe? Is it drowning in debt, living paycheck to paycheck, or being unprepared for emergencies? Jot down these fears – they are the building blocks for your anti-goals. Let's shift our perspective. Instead of letting these fears paralyze us, let's use them as fuel for positive change. Anti-goals are not about dwelling on negativity; they are about transforming fear into motivation and using it as a catalyst for breaking bad financial habits.

Imagine the stress of constantly juggling multiple credit card bills, loans, and living paycheck to paycheck. This is a classic financial fear that many want to avoid. Turning it into an anti-goal means actively working towards eliminating existing debts and avoiding unnecessary ones. The fear of overspending and constantly living beyond one's means is a common concern. Transform this fear into an anti-goal by adopting a frugal mindset, creating and sticking to a budget, and making intentional spending choices.

The anxiety of not having a financial safety net, The thought of reaching retirement age without a solid financial plan, The fear of relying on others for financial support, and the fear of being financially illiterate in a complex world can be overwhelming. Use this fear to set an anti-goal of building and maintaining a robust emergency fund. This fund serves as a buffer against unexpected expenses, providing peace of mind.

For those considering starting a family, the fear of unpreparedness for the financial responsibilities of parenthood is significant. Turn it into an anti-goal by planning and budgeting for childcare, education, and other associated costs.

Now that we've identified some common financial fears and transformed them into anti-goals, let's explore how to turn these anti-goals into actionable steps for positive change.

- Develop and stick to a realistic budget that allocates funds for debt repayment.
- Build an emergency fund to avoid relying on credit in times of crisis
- Allocate a portion of your income to consistently build your emergency fund.

- Set up automatic transfers to your emergency fund to ensure consistent contributions.
- Anticipate potential expenses and adjust your emergency fund accordingly.
- Regularly contribute to retirement accounts, taking advantage of employer matches and tax benefits.
- Diversify investments to mitigate risk and maximize long-term growth
- Invest in your skills and seek opportunities for career advancement.

- Explore side hustles or investments to diversify your sources of income.
- Strive for financial self-sufficiency to reduce dependency on others.
- Dedicate time to reading books, articles, and educational resources on personal finance.
- Participate in workshops, webinars, or seminars focused on financial literacy.

- Develop a comprehensive family plan that includes budgeting for childcare, education, and medical expenses.
- Establish a dedicated fund for your children's education to alleviate future financial burdens.
- Ensure you have adequate insurance coverage to handle unexpected medical expenses.

Anti-goals shine a spotlight on areas of financial vulnerability, promoting heightened awareness. The fear associated with anti-goals serves as a powerful motivator for positive change. It transforms negative emotions into proactive steps, creating a sense of urgency to address and overcome financial challenges. Identifying anti-goals involves acknowledging existing habits that contribute to financial fears.

"I forgive myself for purchasing those expensive Prada shoes"

We've all been there – that sinking feeling when you realize you've made a financial misstep. Whether it's overspending, accumulating debt, or making an investment that didn't quite pan out, the weight of financial regret can be heavy. But what if, instead of carrying that burden indefinitely, you could learn to forgive yourself. Financial forgiveness is a mindset that involves letting go of guilt and self-blame associated with past financial mistakes. It's about acknowledging that everyone makes financial blunders at some point – it's a part of the learning process. The key is to shift the focus from dwelling on the past to using those experiences as stepping stones toward making wiser decisions in the present and future.

Society often perpetuates the idea that financial success is synonymous with perfection – never making a mistake, never overspending, and always having a flawless plan. But let's be real – life is messy, and finances are no exception. When you forgive yourself for financial mistakes, you empower yourself to take control of your financial narrative. It's a declaration that you won't be defined by past missteps but rather by your ability to learn, adapt, and make better choices moving forward. Every mistake is an opportunity for growth. What did you learn from each financial misstep? Perhaps it was the importance of emergency savings, the need for thorough research before an investment, or the value of budgeting.

What steps can you take to rectify the situation or prevent similar mistakes in the future? This could involve adjusting your budget, seeking financial advice, or implementing new saving strategies.

"I will give you my cereal, if you give me some milk"

Money, as we know it, has been deeply ingrained in our societies for centuries. However, with the rise of technological advancements and a growing awareness of sustainability and community, people are exploring alternative currencies that redefine how we exchange value. The traditional concept of money is being challenged by innovative systems that prioritize collaboration, sustainability, and community building.

Let's start with a concept as old as human civilization itself – bartering. Imagine a time when people exchanged goods and services directly without the intermediary of currency. Well, that practice is making a comeback in the form of modern bartering systems. Bartering is the art of swapping goods or services directly without the need for cash. You bring your expertise or your surplus produce to the table, and in return, you get something you need. It's a simple yet powerful way to create a network of interdependence within a community.

Modern bartering platforms facilitate exchanges on a larger scale. Online bartering communities connect individuals with diverse skills and needs, fostering a sense of community. It's not just about getting what you want; it's about building relationships and supporting local talents. The digital revolution has given bartering a new lease on life. Online platforms enable individuals to connect globally, expanding the possibilities for exchange. Whether you're a graphic designer in New York swapping services with a programmer in Tokyo or a farmer in Kenya exchanging produce with a chef in Paris, the potential is vast.

Now, let's shift our focus to an innovative concept known as time banking. Instead of traditional currency, time becomes the currency of exchange in a time banking system. In a time banking system, individuals offer their skills, services, or time to others in exchange for time credits. One hour of your time is equivalent to one time credit, regardless of the service provided. This creates a unique and egalitarian approach to value exchange.

Time banking goes beyond the transactional nature of traditional currency. It emphasizes community collaboration and recognizes the inherent value in each person's skills and time. Whether you're a skilled carpenter or a fantastic cook, your time is seen as valuable, promoting a sense of equality within the community. Time banking has the potential to address social inequality by acknowledging and valuing various skills. In a traditional monetary system, high-income professions are often perceived as more valuable. In a time banking community, all skills are considered equal, creating a more inclusive and supportive environment.

In sharing economies, goods and services are shared or rented among a community, challenging the traditional model of ownership. Sharing economies shift the paradigm from owning assets to accessing them when needed. Whether it's a car, a power tool, or even a vacation home, the emphasis is on shared use rather than individual possession. This not only reduces overall consumption but also promotes sustainability. Companies like Airbnb, Uber, and TaskRabbit connect individuals who have resources or skills with those in need. These platforms act as facilitators, creating a seamless experience for users to share and access goods and services.

The sharing economy relies heavily on community trust. When you're renting out your apartment to a stranger or sharing a ride with someone, trust becomes a cornerstone. This emphasis on trust-building fosters a sense of community and interconnectedness, challenging the transactional nature of traditional markets.

Bartering can coexist with time banking, and both can seamlessly integrate into sharing economies. Imagine a day where you start by bartering – trading your homemade jams for a neighbor's freshly baked bread. Later, you engage in a time banking system, offering your accounting skills to a local community project in exchange for credits. In the evening, you use those credits to access a shared community garden or borrow a power drill from a neighbor through a sharing platform. The common thread in these scenarios is the emphasis on community-centric living. Instead of isolated transactions with faceless entities, individuals are actively engaged in their communities, building relationships and contributing to the well-being of all members. Beyond the social aspects, alternative currencies also have environmental implications. Sharing economies, for instance, reduce the demand for new products, cutting down on resource extraction and waste. This aligns with the growing awareness of the environmental impact of our consumption patterns.

The biggest hurdle is overcoming the ingrained mindset associated with traditional currency. Many people are accustomed to the security and familiarity of using cash or electronic money. Shifting towards alternative currencies requires a change in perception and a willingness to explore new ways of value exchange. Regulatory barriers also pose challenges. Governments and financial institutions are designed around the traditional monetary system. Integrating alternative currencies may require navigating complex regulatory frameworks and overcoming resistance to change. With the rise of decentralized technologies like blockchain, trust in traditional financial institutions is being challenged. However, building trust in decentralized systems requires educating the public on the benefits and addressing concerns related to security and stability.

The Bristol Pound, a local currency in the United Kingdom, encourages spending within the community. Accepted by local businesses, it aims to retain wealth within Bristol, fostering economic resilience and supporting local enterprises. Time Banks USA operates a network of time banks across the country, where individuals exchange services based on time credits. From tutoring to home repairs, this system strengthens community bonds and addresses social needs through a time-based currency.

Freecycle is an online platform where individuals can give away items they no longer need or find things they require, all for free. This sharing platform reduces waste, promotes sustainability, and connects community members based on their shared commitment to environmental stewardship.

Ride-share platforms like Uber and Lyft have revolutionized transportation by turning personal vehicles into shared resources. This not only reduces the number of individual cars on the road but also creates economic opportunities for drivers and promotes community collaboration.

"I'm allergic to spending, but only for a week"

Imagine hitting pause on your spending habits for a whole week—no swiping cards, no online shopping, just a financial fasting challenge. So, what exactly is financial fasting? It's a conscious decision to refrain from spending money for a specific period. It's about challenging your spending impulses, reevaluating your needs versus wants, and tapping into the resources already at your disposal.

The first day is all about transitioning into the mindset of financial fasting. You wake up, excited and a bit apprehensive, realizing that the week ahead is going to be different. The key here is to set clear intentions and goals for the week. What do you want to achieve? Is it saving money, breaking a spending habit, or simply gaining a deeper understanding of your relationship with money?

Start by taking stock of what you already have. Look into your pantry, fridge, and any other essentials. This exercise not only helps you plan your meals for the week but also highlights how much you already possess. Identify non-essential spending triggers. Whether it's that daily cup of fancy coffee or impulse online purchases, understanding your spending habits allows you to prepare mentally for the challenges ahead.

Establish your essential needs for the week—things you cannot go without. This might include groceries, transportation for work, or necessary bills. Clearly defining these needs helps you distinguish between essential and non-essential spending. Devote time to planning meals and activities for the week. By preparing in advance, you minimize the temptation to spend on convenience. Pack lunch, plan simple and cost-effective dinners, and identify free or low-cost activities for leisure.

As you step into the middle of the week, you'll likely encounter a few challenges and temptations. It's crucial to stay focused on your goals and adapt to unexpected situations. If grocery shopping is a must, approach it with a purpose. Stick to your list of essential items, and resist the urge to grab those tempting snacks or extras. Financial fasting is not about deprivation but about conscious choices.

Social engagements can be tricky during financial fasting. Instead of avoiding friends or canceling plans, suggest low-cost or free activities. Consider a potluck dinner, a picnic in the park, or a game night at home. Communicate openly with your friends about your financial fasting challenge. The temptation to spend may arise unexpectedly. Maybe you pass by your favorite café, or there's a tempting online sale. Acknowledge the temptation, but remind yourself of the goals you set at the beginning of the week. Explore the myriad of free activities available in your community. From hiking and biking to visiting local museums on free admission days, there are often plenty of ways to enjoy your leisure time without spending money.

Midway through the week, you're likely discovering a newfound sense of resourcefulness. You've become more mindful of your spending triggers and are finding creative ways to meet your needs without reaching for your wallet. By now, you've probably mastered the art of creating meals from what you have. Get creative with your cooking—experiment with new recipes using the ingredients you already own. Not only does this save money, but it can also be a fun and rewarding experience.

If transportation is a potential expense, explore alternative options. Consider carpooling with colleagues, biking, or using public transportation. Financial fasting isn't just about saving money; it's about finding sustainable alternatives to spending

Use this time to reevaluate your priorities. Are there subscriptions or memberships that you can live without? The financial fasting experience can reveal hidden expenses and help you reassess what truly adds value to your life.

Engage with your local community during financial fasting. Attend free community events, participate in volunteer activities, or join local groups that align with your interests. Connecting with others can be fulfilling and cost-free.

As you approach the end of the financial fasting week, it's time to reflect on the challenges and victories you've encountered. Celebrate your achievements, no matter how small, and consider how this experience might shape your relationship with money.

Financial fasting heightens your awareness of spending patterns. By deliberately abstaining from spending, you become more mindful of your financial decisions, distinguishing between needs and wants. The experience cultivates resourcefulness. Whether it's creatively using ingredients from your pantry or finding alternative transportation options, financial fasting encourages you to tap into your resourcefulness and think outside the spending box

As your week of financial fasting concludes, it's not just an end but a beginning—an opportunity to carry forward the lessons learned into your everyday life. Financial fasting is not about adopting a permanent state of deprivation but about cultivating a conscious and intentional relationship with money.

"Hello dear, so, em… wanna talk about my finances?"

We all know it – money talk has this unspoken, somewhat uncomfortable air around it. People tend to keep their financial struggles and goals close to the chest. But what if we challenge that norm? The first step is acknowledging the taboo. We've been conditioned to keep our financial struggles private, but it's time to challenge that notion. By breaking the silence, we create space for understanding, support, and shared experiences. Keeping financial struggles hidden can be like carrying a heavy burden. It's isolating, and the weight of it can impact not just your bank account but your mental well-being. Sharing that load with someone you trust can be liberating. Financial challenges are a part of life for many, and discussing them openly can help break down the stigma. When we realize that others face similar struggles, it becomes easier to navigate our own financial journey.

Now, let's talk about those trusted friends or family members. The ones you know have your back no matter what. Opening up to them about your financial situation might be nerve-wracking, but it's a crucial step toward building a support system. Not everyone needs to know your financial details. Start by choosing a small circle of people you trust – friends or family members who have demonstrated empathy, understanding, and a non-judgmental attitude. When you decide to open up, set the tone for the conversation. Make it clear that you're sharing not to seek pity but to gain support and accountability. It's a brave step, and framing it positively can encourage a constructive dialogue. Vulnerability isn't just about admitting struggles; it's about sharing the entire journey, the highs and the lows.

Don't shy away from expressing the emotional impact of your financial situation. Whether it's stress, anxiety, or the weight of uncertainty, being open about how money affects your emotions can deepen understanding. As you open up, you might be surprised to find that those you confide in have their own financial stories. Shared experiences can be a powerful catalyst for connection and mutual support. Financial struggles are often more common than we think. When you share your challenges, you might discover that others have faced similar situations. This realization can foster empathy and create a sense of shared struggle.

Embracing financial vulnerability is a two-way street. As you share your experiences, be open to learning from others. They might offer insights, advice, or perspectives that you hadn't considered. It's a collective journey toward financial wisdom.

Your confidantes become part of your support network. They are there not just to lend a listening ear but to provide encouragement, advice, and even accountability as you work towards your financial goals. A problem shared is a problem halved.

The more we open up about our financial experiences, the more we contribute to breaking down stigmas surrounding money. It becomes a step towards a more transparent and compassionate society where individuals can support each other in their financial journeys.

One of the main reasons people hesitate to talk about money is the fear of judgment. Will they think I'm irresponsible? Will they look down on me? Remember, vulnerability is not weakness. It's strength. It takes courage to share your truth. Opening up about financial struggles fosters empathy, not judgment. The people who care about you are likely to respond with understanding and a desire to help. This creates a supportive environment where everyone can share their burdens and triumphs.

When introducing the topic, frame it in a positive light. Emphasize that you see this as an opportunity for growth and improvement and that you value their input and support. You don't have to reveal every detail in the first conversation. Share what you're comfortable with, and gauge the response. As trust deepens, you can choose to disclose more specifics. Encourage a two-way conversation by asking for input and advice. This not only makes the conversation more collaborative but also shows that you value their perspectives. Expect questions, and be open to answering them. Your confidantes might need more information to fully understand your situation and provide meaningful support. Always express gratitude for their willingness to listen and support you. Acknowledge that this is a vulnerable topic, and their support means a lot to you.

"If it's taking your time, there has to be a financial end-goal"

Here's something that might not be on your mind every day but is crucial for the long game – having a financial exit strategy. Whether you're knee-deep in a career, running a business, or investing in a passion project, planning your financial exit is like having something to look forward to that makes it all worth it. It's like having a safety net when you're walking on a tightrope – you hope you won't fall, but just in case, you've got a plan.

Life is unpredictable, and things change. Your career might take a turn, your business landscape could shift, or your personal goals might evolve. An exit strategy helps you adapt to change without financial chaos. Whether you've invested time, money, or both, having an exit strategy safeguards your investments. It ensures that your efforts and resources are protected, even if circumstances lead you to change direction. Ironically, having an exit plan can open doors to new opportunities. It allows you to close one chapter intentionally, making room for fresh endeavors or focusing on what truly matters to you. At the core, a financial exit strategy is about securing your financial well-being. It's the difference between scrambling for stability and gracefully transitioning to the next phase of your life.

If you're an entrepreneur, selling your business could be a strategic exit. This might involve finding a buyer or merging with another company. The goal is to extract value from your business and secure a profitable exit

On the professional side, a career transition could be your exit strategy. This might involve moving to a different industry, starting a new role, or even launching your own venture. The key is to transition smoothly without compromising your financial stability. If you're heavily invested in stocks, real estate, or other ventures, your exit strategy could involve divesting or selling those assets at a favorable period. This ensures that you realize the returns on your investments and manage any associated risks. In some cases, your exit strategy might involve passing the baton. This could mean grooming a successor in your business or mentorship in your profession. The idea is to leave a legacy and ensure continuity in your absence. A classic exit strategy is retirement planning.

"Hey kid! I'm doing a survey. How do you save, spend, and invest?"

We often associate mentorship with the idea of learning from those who have more experience, more years in the game. But what if we turned that concept on its head and tapped into the fresh perspectives of the younger generation? The world is changing faster than ever, and the younger generation is at the forefront of this change. Their approach to money reflects the evolving landscape of digital currencies, gig economies, and unconventional career paths. By embracing reverse mentorship, we can gain valuable insights into navigating this dynamic terrain.

Younger individuals are often more tech-savvy, having grown up in the digital age. Their comfort with online tools, apps, and innovative financial technologies can shed light on efficient ways to manage money, track expenses, and invest wisely. The younger generation is known for its entrepreneurial spirit. Whether it's launching side hustles, exploring the gig economy, or embracing the sharing economy, their mindset towards earning and saving money can inspire us to think outside the traditional financial box. Unlike previous generations that might have prioritized material possessions, younger individuals often value experiences over things. This shift in priorities can offer valuable perspectives on budgeting, saving, and investing with an emphasis on creating meaningful life experiences.

Younger individuals bring fresh perspectives to the table. Their approach to money management, budgeting, and investing might incorporate innovative tools and strategies that the older generation might not be as familiar with. The younger generation is often more adaptable to change, especially when it comes to embracing new technologies. Learning from their experiences can help older individuals navigate the evolving landscape of personal finance. Younger individuals are more likely to leverage automation and technology in managing their finances. This can be a game-changer in terms of efficiency and accuracy.

While reverse mentorship in personal finance offers valuable insights, it's essential to acknowledge potential challenges and considerations. Younger individuals may not have the same financial responsibilities or complexities as their older counterparts. This difference in financial situations can impact the relevance of certain advice and strategies.

Risk tolerance and financial goals can vary significantly based on life stages. It's crucial to align the advice received through reverse mentorship with individual risk preferences and long-term objectives.

Cultural and generational differences can influence financial perspectives. It's important to approach reverse mentorship with an open mind, recognizing that what works for one person might not necessarily apply universally. While embracing innovation and fresh perspectives, it's equally important to value the experience and wisdom of those who have weathered economic shifts and financial challenges. A balanced approach that integrates the best of both worlds is ideal.

Reverse mentorship in personal finance is not about age; it's about learning and growing together. The exchange of ideas, experiences, and perspectives can enrich our understanding of money and how we relate to it.

"This $5 has a psychology? Wait... I'm being controlled?"

Money is more than just a medium of exchange; it's a powerful force that influences our thoughts, emotions, and behaviors. It can represent security, power, freedom, success, or even self-worth. Our emotions and money are deeply entwined. From the exhilaration of a financial windfall to the anxiety of debt, each monetary event triggers emotional responses. The society we grow up in and the cultural values we inherit shape our financial attitudes. Messages about money from family, media, and societal norms create a blueprint that influences our financial decisions. Behavioral economics explores the psychological factors that impact economic decisions. Concepts like loss aversion, mental accounting, and the influence of social norms shed light on why we make certain financial choices, often deviating from rational economic behavior.

In many households, money is not just a means of exchange; it's a symbol of security, success, or even love. Parents who constantly worry about money may inadvertently instill a sense of financial anxiety in their children. On the other hand, those who view money as a measure of success may foster a drive for material wealth.

These early impressions create money scripts—unspoken rules and beliefs about money that shape our financial behaviors. Some people may adopt a scarcity mindset, constantly fearing that there won't be enough, while others embrace an abundance mentality, believing that opportunities for wealth are limitless.

A sudden raise at work may lead to feelings of accomplishment and validation, while job loss can evoke fear, shame, and even a sense of identity crisis.

Financial stress is a common emotional companion in the modern world. The pressure to meet financial obligations, coupled with societal expectations and the desire for a certain lifestyle, can create a perfect storm of stress and anxiety. This emotional burden can spill over into other areas of life, affecting relationships, physical health, and overall well-being.

Interestingly, the psychological impact of money is not always proportional to the amount one possesses. A person with substantial wealth may experience financial anxiety, fearing loss or grappling with the responsibility that comes with wealth. On the flip side, someone with limited resources may find contentment and peace, viewing wealth as a state of mind rather than a number in the bank.

Our relationship with money is intricately tied to our sense of self-worth and identity. In a consumer-driven society, possessions and wealth are often equated with success and social status. This external validation can lead to a perpetual pursuit of more, as individuals strive to keep up with societal expectations and maintain a certain image.

Conversely, financial setbacks can trigger a crisis of identity. Job loss or financial failure may prompt individuals to question their worth and competence. In extreme cases, it can lead to feelings of shame and inadequacy, eroding one's self-esteem.

The link between money and identity is not just about societal pressures. Personal values and beliefs also play a crucial role. Some may find purpose and fulfillment in philanthropy, using their wealth to make a positive impact on the world. Others may derive satisfaction from financial independence and the ability to live life on their own terms.

Our spending habits are often a direct reflection of our emotional state. Retail therapy, for example, is a common phenomenon where individuals seek comfort or distraction through shopping. The temporary high of making a purchase can provide a momentary escape from stress or negative emotions.

Conversely, financial restraint can be a form of self-discipline or a response to feelings of guilt or fear. A person who grew up in a financially unstable environment may develop a strong aversion to debt and become an avid saver, seeking security in financial independence.

Understanding these emotional triggers can help individuals gain control over their spending patterns.

The curated online personas of friends, celebrities, and influencers showcase luxurious lifestyles, exotic vacations, and expensive possessions. Constant exposure to these images can fuel feelings of inadequacy and the desire for more.

The phenomenon of "keeping up with the Joneses" has evolved into a global scale competition. People may find themselves chasing after a lifestyle that is not sustainable or authentic to their values, solely to meet societal expectations. This external focus can lead to a perpetual cycle of dissatisfaction, as there will always be someone with a bigger house, a nicer car, or a more glamorous life.

The fear of scarcity is a powerful psychological force that drives many financial decisions. Whether rooted in childhood experiences or societal conditioning, the belief that there's never enough can lead to hoarding, excessive frugality, and an inability to enjoy the present.

This scarcity mindset can be a self-fulfilling prophecy. Constantly dwelling on what might be lacking can hinder opportunities for growth and success. It can also strain relationships, as the fear of scarcity may lead to a reluctance to share resources or collaborate with others.

Overcoming the scarcity mindset involves cultivating a mindset of abundance. This shift in perspective acknowledges the potential for growth, opportunities, and collaboration. It allows individuals to approach life with optimism and openness, fostering a healthier relationship with money.

"I just finished listening to your rants; that would be $150 please. My time is valuable"

You're in need of some help assembling that intimidating piece of furniture that arrived in a flat-pack nightmare. Or perhaps your unruly garden has declared its independence, and you desperately need someone with green thumbs (or, let's be honest, anyone with thumbs) to tame the wilderness. What if I told you there's a way to get these tasks done without spending a dime?

So, time banking isn't a futuristic concept involving time travel or some elaborate clockwork barter system. It's a simple, community-driven idea that revolves around the principle that everyone's time is valuable, and skills are a form of treasure waiting to be unearthed. Instead of waving cash around like it's going out of style, you're waving your skills in a friendly exchange with others.

Let's say you're a whiz in the kitchen, capable of turning a can of beans into a gourmet masterpiece. Meanwhile, your neighbor Steve is a DIY maestro with the ability to fix just about anything. In the world of time banking, you can offer Steve a cooking lesson, complete with secret spice revelations, in exchange for him rescuing your wobbly kitchen table from a certain demise. It's a win-win, and no money needs to exchange hands—just a bit of friendly banter and perhaps a few laughs along the way.

you might be wondering how this all works. Is there a secret handshake or a club you need to join? Fear not, intrepid time banker! The beauty of time banking lies in its simplicity.

First things first, you need to identify your skills and talents. Maybe you're a pro at pet grooming, a computer whiz, or an expert at untangling the mess that is a teenager's bedroom. List these skills out; this is your time currency.

Next, connect with your community—friends, neighbors, or that person you always nod at but never really spoke to because, let's be honest, adult friendships are like dating without the awkward dinners. Float the idea of time banking, and you'll likely find a surprising number of people interested in swapping skills instead of dollars.

Platforms and apps are also jumping on the time banking bandwagon, making it easier to connect with like-minded individuals. It's like Tinder but for skill exchanges. Swipe right for someone who can teach you how to salsa dance, and in return, teach them how to cook the perfect omelet. Who knows, you might end up with a dance party brunch extravaganza.

You might stumble upon Mary, who's a yoga guru in the making, willing to trade her expertise for your graphic design skills. Suddenly, your quest for inner peace just got a lot more visually appealing, and Mary is on her way to having a logo that could rival the Mona Lisa (or at least make her neighborhood yoga class look pretty snazzy). A variety of services can be exchanged. Language lessons, gardening tips, dog walking, resume writing—you name it! If you've got a skill, there's probably someone out there looking to trade their unique talent for yours. It's like having your own personal Craigslist, minus the shady dealings and questionable meet-up locations.

Let's look at the delicate aspect of negotiation in time banking. It's not about haggling over prices; it's about finding a fair exchange that leaves everyone feeling like they've struck gold in this skill-sharing adventure.

Imagine you're negotiating with Brian, who's a seasoned handyman and has the uncanny ability to fix leaky faucets with just a stern look. You, on the other hand, are a pro at organizing chaotic spaces, transforming cluttered rooms into havens of serenity.

As you engage in this barter banter, throw in a quip like, "I'll organize your toolbox, and you won't need a map to find the right screwdriver anymore. In return, I expect leak-free faucet magic for at least a year. Deal?" Laughter not only eases the negotiation process but also makes the exchange feel more like a friendly favor than a transaction.

One of the unexpected perks of time banking is the sense of community it fosters. In a world that often feels more digitally connected but emotionally distant, time banking brings people together for real, face-to-face interactions. It's a chance to break down the barriers that can separate us in our busy lives and discover the hidden talents within our own neighborhoods.

Think about it: You might have lived next to Jenny for years, exchanged nods during the occasional mailbox encounter, but never really knew that she's an undiscovered painting prodigy. Time banking creates opportunities to unlock these hidden gems and build a stronger, more connected community.

And let's not forget the potential for community events. Imagine a skill-sharing fair where everyone sets up booths showcasing their talents. You could have a booth for "Learn to Juggle Like a Pro" next to "Financial Planning 101." It's like a carnival, but with life skills instead of cotton candy (although, who's to say you can't have both?).

Of course, like any endeavor, time banking has its quirks and challenges. One potential pitfall is the classic "awkward encounter" scenario. You know the one—when you realize you've asked your neighbor to teach you how to play the ukulele, but they don't actually own a ukulele. To avoid these moments, communication is key. Clearly outline what you're offering and what you hope to receive in return. If your potential time banking buddy doesn't have the skills you're looking for, no harm done. Just laugh it off and maybe suggest they learn the ukulele for future exchanges. You never know when a spontaneous ukulele jam might come in handy.

Another challenge is the temptation to overcommit. You're so excited about the prospect of learning salsa dancing, French cooking, and car maintenance that you agree to everything. Suddenly, your calendar looks like a game of Tetris, and you're wondering when you'll find time to sleep. The key here is to pace yourself. Remember, time banking is meant to enhance your life, not turn it into a whirlwind of activities. Start with a few exchanges, see how it goes, and then expand your horizons. It's like trying a new cuisine—you wouldn't order the entire menu on your first visit, would you? Well, maybe you would, but you get the point.

"I am wealthier than my colleague in everything… except money"

You meet someone new, and one of the first questions that typically pops up is, "What do you do for a living?" It's as if our professions define our worth. We've been conditioned to measure success by the size of our paychecks, the prestige of our job titles, and the luxury of our possessions. But, is this really the true essence of a prosperous life? What if we challenge these norms? What if we question the conventional wisdom that success is directly proportional to wealth and material accumulation? In doing so, we open up a space for redefining our priorities, values, and ultimately, our sense of financial well-being.

Financial well-being should extend beyond the mere accumulation of wealth. It's a holistic concept that encompasses financial security, fulfillment, and a sense of purpose. Instead of pursuing wealth for its own sake, let's explore a more profound understanding of financial well-being—one that considers personal happiness, community engagement, and the pursuit of passions.

What if, instead of accumulating material possessions, we shifted our focus to accumulating experiences? The joy of a shared meal with loved ones, the thrill of exploring new places, or the satisfaction of contributing to a cause larger than ourselves—these are the moments that truly enrich our lives. By valuing experiences over possessions, we can redefine our relationship with money and success. Social media exacerbates the pressure to conform to societal norms around wealth and success. Scrolling through curated feeds, it's easy to feel inadequate compared to others who flaunt their seemingly perfect lives. But what if we acknowledged that these images often represent a curated reality, not the whole story?

Success is a deeply personal concept, and its definition should be as diverse as humanity itself. It's about time we detach success from the traditional markers of wealth and prestige and look inward to define what it means to us individually. Success could be achieving work-life balance, pursuing a passion, or making a positive impact in our communities.

"Multiple income streams is how millionaires are made"

Imagine your career as a portfolio of different projects, gigs, and business ventures, much like a financial investment portfolio. Instead of relying solely on a single job, you spread your professional endeavors across various areas. It's like having multiple safety nets, and if one part of your portfolio takes a hit, the others can help balance things out. You've probably heard it in the context of investments, right? Well, the same principle applies to your career. By diversifying your income streams, you reduce the risk associated with depending on a single source of income. It's like planting different crops in your garden – if one doesn't do well, the others might flourish.

One way to diversify your income is by exploring freelancing and side hustles. Whether you're a graphic designer, writer, programmer, or have any skill in demand, platforms like Upwork, Fiverr, and Freelancer offer a plethora of opportunities. These gigs not only bring in extra cash but also allow you to showcase your skills to a broader audience. A portfolio career encourages entrepreneurship. It could be a small online store, a consulting agency, or even a tech startup. Building a business from the ground up not only adds another income stream but also nurtures your creativity and resilience.

Time is your most valuable asset in a portfolio career. Plan your days meticulously, allocating specific blocks of time to each project or venture. Tools like calendars, project management apps, and good old to-do lists can be your best friends in this journey. Also, all gigs and ventures are not created equal. Some will demand more attention than others. Identify your priorities and focus on the projects that align with your long-term goals. This doesn't mean neglecting the smaller gigs; it's about strategic prioritization.

Here's a list of multiple streams of income for anyone hoping to increase their income portfolio:

Income Stream	Description
1. Full-Time Job	A traditional nine-to-five job in your chosen field. Provides a stable and consistent source of income.
2. Freelancing Gigs	Offer your skills on platforms like Upwork, Fiverr, or Freelancer. Examples include writing, graphic design, programming, and more.
3. Side Hustles	Small businesses or projects you run on the side. This could include selling handmade crafts, offering consulting services, or tutoring.
4. Entrepreneurship	Start your own business, whether it's an online store, a consulting agency, a food delivery service, or a tech startup.
5. Real Estate	Invest in real estate properties to generate

Income Stream	Description
Income	rental income or profit from property appreciation.
6. Stock Market	Invest in stocks, bonds, or mutual funds to benefit from market growth and dividends. Requires some financial knowledge and risk tolerance.
7. Dividend Income	Invest in dividend-paying stocks to receive regular dividend payments. A form of passive income.
8. Affiliate Marketing	Promote other people's products and earn a commission for every sale made through your unique affiliate link.
9. Online Courses	Create and sell online courses on platforms like Udemy or Teachable, sharing your expertise in a particular subject.
10.	Start a blog or YouTube channel. Monetize

Income Stream	Description
Blogging/Vlogging	through ads, sponsorships, affiliate marketing, and merchandise sales.
11. Rental Income	Rent out assets you own, such as a room on Airbnb, equipment, or even your car through platforms like Turo.
12. Virtual Assistance	Offer administrative support services to businesses or entrepreneurs remotely.
13. Social Media Management	Manage social media accounts for businesses or individuals, helping them grow their online presence.
14. App Development	Create and monetize mobile applications. This requires programming skills or collaboration with a developer.
15. Photography	Sell your photos to stock photo websites or offer photography services for events, portraits, or commercial purposes.

Income Stream	Description
16. E-commerce	Set up an online store and sell products. This could involve dropshipping, creating handmade goods, or selling digital products.
17. Fitness Coaching	Become a certified fitness coach and offer personalized training sessions or create online fitness programs.
18. Consulting Services	Provide consulting services in your area of expertise, such as business, marketing, career, or financial consulting.
19. Virtual Events Hosting	Host webinars, workshops, or virtual events and monetize through ticket sales or sponsorships.
20. Podcasting	Start a podcast and monetize through sponsorships, ads, listener donations, or exclusive content for paid subscribers.
Income Stream	Description

Income Stream	Description
21. Remote Job Opportunities	Explore remote job opportunities in various fields, allowing you to work from anywhere with an internet connection.
22. Affiliate Sales	Promote products through affiliate programs on your blog, social media, or website and earn a commission for each sale made through your referral link.
23. Online Surveys and Reviews	Participate in paid online surveys, review products, or join platforms that pay for your opinion on products and services.
24. Cryptocurrency Investments	Invest in cryptocurrencies, such as Bitcoin or Ethereum, and potentially benefit from price appreciation or trading strategies.
25. Remote Tutoring	Offer tutoring services in subjects you excel at or provide assistance with test preparation for students through online platforms.

Income Stream	Description
26. Create and Sell Art	If you have artistic talents, create and sell artwork, digital art, or even custom designs on platforms like Etsy or through your own website.
27. Rent Out Your Vehicle	Utilize services like Turo to rent out your vehicle when you're not using it, turning your car into a source of passive income.
28. Write and Self-Publish Books	Write and publish e-books or physical books on platforms like Amazon Kindle Direct Publishing or other self-publishing services.
29. Language Translation Services	If you're fluent in multiple languages, offer translation services for documents, websites, or even act as an interpreter for meetings.
30. Stock Photography	Sell your high-quality photos to stock photography websites, allowing businesses and individuals to purchase and use your

Income Stream	Description
	images.
31. Social Media Influencing	Build a strong social media presence and collaborate with brands for sponsored content, product placements, or brand ambassadorships.
32. Develop Online Software Tools	Create and sell software tools, plugins, or apps that address specific needs or challenges in industries such as business, design, or productivity.
33. Create and Sell Digital Products	Develop and sell digital products like templates, printables, or design assets on platforms such as Gumroad or Etsy.
34. Remote Customer Service	Work as a remote customer service representative for companies that outsource their customer support functions.
35. Subscription	Curate and sell subscription boxes with niche

Income Stream	Description
Box Services	products or experiences, catering to specific interests or hobbies.
36. Rent Your Equipment	If you own specialized equipment (e.g., camera gear, power tools), consider renting it out to others in your community or through online platforms.
37. Create an Online Course Marketplace	Build a platform that allows instructors to sell and promote their online courses, earning a commission for each course sold.
38. Health and Wellness Coaching	Become a certified health or wellness coach, providing personalized guidance on nutrition, fitness, and overall well-being.
39. Virtual Assistance for Events	Offer virtual event planning and coordination services, assisting individuals or businesses in organizing successful online events.
40. Create and	Design and sell branded merchandise related

Income Stream	Description
Sell Merchandise	to your personal brand, business, or niche interests through print-on-demand services.

Income Stream	Description
41. Mystery Shopping	Get paid to visit stores, restaurants, or businesses anonymously and provide feedback on your experience.
42. Teach a Skill	If you have expertise in a particular skill, offer online or in-person classes. This could include music lessons, language tutoring, or coding workshops.
43. Personal Chef/Catering	If you're a skilled cook, offer personal chef services or catering for events, parties, or individuals who appreciate homemade meals.
44. Affiliate Dropshipping	Combine affiliate marketing with dropshipping by creating an e-commerce store and promoting products for a commission without

Income Stream	Description
	handling inventory.
45. Rent Your Space	Rent out unused space in your home or property for events, photo shoots, storage, or even as a co-working space.
46. Invest in Crowdfunding Projects	Participate in crowdfunding platforms that allow you to invest in startups, real estate, or creative projects in exchange for potential returns.
47. Subscription-Based Content	Create premium content on platforms like Patreon or Substack, offering exclusive material to subscribers who pay a monthly fee.
48. Remote IT Support	Provide remote IT support services for individuals or small businesses experiencing technical issues with their computers or networks.
49. Flip Items	Buy and sell second-hand items for a profit.

Income Stream	Description
	This could include thrift store finds, antiques, or refurbished electronics.
50. Develop and Sell WordPress Themes	Create and sell custom WordPress themes to website owners and businesses looking for unique and professionally designed templates.
51. Digital Marketing Services	Offer digital marketing services such as social media management, SEO optimization, or content creation for businesses seeking an online presence.
52. Travel Blogging/Vlogging	Combine your love for travel with income by documenting your journeys through a blog or YouTube channel, monetizing through sponsorships and travel-related partnerships.
53. Coding Bootcamps	If you're skilled in programming, organize coding bootcamps or workshops to teach others coding skills and software

Income Stream	Description
	development.
54. Develop and Sell Mobile Apps	Create and sell mobile applications on platforms like the App Store or Google Play, catering to specific needs or providing entertainment.
55. Remote Data Entry	Offer remote data entry services to businesses or individuals who require assistance in managing and organizing their data.
56. Social Media Consultancy	Provide consulting services to businesses looking to enhance their social media presence, strategy, and engagement with their target audience.
57. Pet Sitting/Dog Walking	If you love animals, offer pet sitting or dog walking services to pet owners in your community.
58. Online	Monetize your passion for gaming by

Income Stream	Description
Gaming and Streaming	streaming on platforms like Twitch, creating content on YouTube, or participating in esports tournaments.
59. Sustainable Living Coaching	Become a coach or consultant for individuals or businesses looking to adopt more sustainable and eco-friendly practices.
60. Develop and Sell 3D Models	If you have 3D modeling skills, create and sell digital 3D models for use in animations, games, or virtual reality applications.

"The Keyword is Financial self-care"

Imagine taking care of your mental and emotional well-being without burning a hole in your wallet. It's all about prioritizing activities that not only enrich your life but also nurture your financial health. Let's start by unpacking the idea of financial self-care. At its core, it's about recognizing the deep connection between your financial health and overall well-being. Just like you'd invest time and energy in physical or mental self-care, financial self-care involves intentional actions that contribute to your financial wellness. The beauty of it? It doesn't require a hefty budget; in fact, it's all about embracing activities that are either free or come at a minimal cost.

Stress about money matters can take a toll on your mental and physical health. Financial self-care aims to break this cycle by promoting a healthy relationship with money and fostering a positive mindset. Nature has a magical way of grounding us and putting things into perspective. Take a stroll in the park, hike a nearby trail, or simply sit in a garden. Connecting with nature is a form of financial self-care that costs nothing but offers priceless moments of tranquility. It's a reset button for your mind, allowing you to approach financial challenges with a clearer perspective.

Affirmations are like mini pep talks for your subconscious mind. Integrate positive financial affirmations into your daily routine.

Whether you say them aloud or write them down, affirmations can shift your mindset from scarcity to abundance.

Example Affirmations:

"I am in control of my finances, and money flows to me effortlessly."

"Every dollar I spend comes back to me multiplied."

Who said self-care has to come in a fancy package? Create your own spa day at home with DIY facemasks, a bubble bath, and calming music. It's a luxurious experience without the hefty price. Planning your meals not only contributes to your physical health but also saves you money. Cook in batches, embrace leftovers, and explore affordable yet nutritious recipes. The bonus? You'll likely eat out less, contributing to significant savings.

Thrifting isn't just a trend; it's a sustainable and budget-friendly lifestyle. From clothing to furniture, consider secondhand options. Not only will you save money, but you'll also contribute to reducing waste.

Joining or creating a money support group can be a game-changer. Share financial goals, challenges, and victories with like-minded individuals. It's a safe space to learn, grow, and hold each other accountable.

"Welcome to the coven. It's a dark, misty night...therefore, we shall only discuss finance!"

We've all heard the saying, "You are the average of the five people you spend the most time with." Well, this holds true for your financial well-being as well. Your inner circle plays a significant role in shaping your attitudes, habits, and perspectives regarding money. In a financially conscious community, learning becomes a collaborative effort. Everyone brings unique experiences, insights, and knowledge to the table. It's like having a round-the-clock financial think tank where you can tap into the collective wisdom to navigate challenges and explore innovative solutions.

Seek out individuals with diverse financial perspectives. This includes people at different stages of their financial journey, those with varied income levels, and individuals with expertise in different aspects of personal finance. A diverse group provides a well-rounded view of money management strategies. Positivity is contagious. Look for individuals who approach financial challenges with a growth-oriented mindset. This doesn't mean ignoring obstacles but viewing them as opportunities for learning and improvement. A positive mindset can be a powerful motivator during both good and challenging times.

"When I get to level 5, I'll have a cheeseburger"

When you turn tasks into a game, you tap into the intrinsic human desire for challenge, accomplishment, and reward. It transforms mundane activities into engaging pursuits, making the road to financial success not only more enjoyable but also more sustainable. Imagine approaching your financial goals like levels in a game. Challenges are the quests you embark on to conquer each level, making the journey more exciting and dynamic. Whether it's saving a certain amount, reducing debt, or increasing your income, set specific and realistic challenges that push you just enough to keep things interesting.

What's a game without rewards? Attach rewards to your financial achievements to make the journey even more satisfying. Rewards could be anything from a small treat, a guilt-free splurge, or a fun experience. The key is to make the rewards proportional to the challenge or milestone, creating a sense of accomplishment and enjoyment.

Just like choosing a game genre, decide what financial game suits you best. Are you more inclined towards a role-playing game where you conquer financial challenges to earn points and rewards? Or perhaps a strategy game where you plan your financial moves strategically to achieve long-term goals? Pick a game style that aligns with your personality and motivates you.

In gaming, quests drive the storyline and keep players engaged. Translate this concept to your finances by defining your quests or challenges. These could be short-term goals like reducing discretionary spending, finding a side hustle, or negotiating bills. The key is to make these quests specific, measurable, and achievable within a set timeframe.

"Craft your own money rules"

For years, we've been bombarded with standard advice – save 15% of your income, invest in a diversified portfolio, avoid debt like the plague. While these guidelines have merit, they don't always capture the nuances of individual lives. Traditional financial advice often adopts a one-size-fits-all mentality. It assumes that everyone's financial circumstances, goals, and values are identical. But in reality, our financial lives are as unique as our fingerprints. Your path may involve unconventional aspirations, distinct challenges, or alternative paths to success that traditional advice doesn't fully acknowledge.

The rise of gig economies, changing job markets, and technological advancements have reshaped the way we earn, spend, and invest. Traditional advice, while timeless in many aspects, might not always align with the evolving financial realities of the 21st century. No two financial journeys are identical. Your circumstances, aspirations, and challenges are distinct to you. By creating custom money rules, you tailor your financial strategies to fit your unique circumstances. Whether you're a freelancer with irregular income or a digital nomad with a global lifestyle, your rules should be a reflection of your reality.

Life is unpredictable, and your financial rules should be flexible enough to adapt to changing circumstances.

Here are a few examples of personal finance rules to get you started. You can use these as motivation to create as many rules as you want:

1. **The 50/30/20 Rule:**

Traditional Rule: Allocate 50% of your income to needs, 30% to wants, and 20% to savings.

Personalized Rule: Adjust the percentages based on your priorities. If you're in a high-cost living area, you might need to allocate more to needs. If savings is a top priority, consider shifting more towards the savings category.

2. **Emergency Fund Rule:**

Traditional Rule: Save three to six months' worth of living expenses in an emergency fund.

Personalized Rule: Customize the emergency fund based on your job stability, industry, and risk tolerance. Freelancers or those with variable income might aim for a larger emergency fund.

3. **Investment Diversification Rule:**

Traditional Rule: Diversify investments across different asset classes to reduce risk.

Personalized Rule: Consider your risk tolerance, investment goals, and interests. If you're passionate about a specific industry or believe in a particular type of investment, adjust your diversification strategy accordingly.

4. **Debt Repayment Rule:**

Traditional Rule: Prioritize high-interest debt repayment.

Personalized Rule: While high-interest debt should be a priority, consider the emotional impact of different debts. Some may prefer to pay off smaller debts first for psychological wins, even if the interest rate is lower.

5. **Budgeting Rule:**

Traditional Rule: Track every expense meticulously and create a detailed budget.

Personalized Rule: Choose a budgeting method that suits your lifestyle. It could be a zero-based budget, a percentage-based budget, or a more relaxed approach like tracking trends over time. The goal is to find a system that you can stick to consistently.

6. Retirement Savings Rule:

Traditional Rule: Save 15% of your income for retirement.

Personalized Rule: Assess your retirement goals, considering factors like desired lifestyle, retirement age, and other income sources. You might need to save more or less depending on your unique circumstances.

7. Credit Card Rule:

Traditional Rule: Avoid credit card debt at all costs.

Personalized Rule: If you can use credit cards responsibly, consider leveraging them for rewards and cashback. Automate payments to avoid interest and fees.

8. Side Hustle Rule:

Traditional Rule: Consider a side hustle to boost income.

Personalized Rule: Tailor your side hustle to your skills, passions, and time availability. It doesn't have to be a traditional part-time job; it could be monetizing a hobby or freelance work.

9. Housing Rule:

Traditional Rule: Spend no more than 30% of your income on housing.

Personalized Rule: Adjust the percentage based on your location and priorities. If living in a high-cost area is essential to you, you might allocate a larger percentage to housing.

Craft your rules by drawing inspiration and insight from money habits and financial mistakes that people make just too often. Here is a list of the money mistakes that are very popular:

1. Living beyond means: Spending more money than earned.
2. Impulse buying: Making unplanned purchases without considering long-term consequences.
3. Emotional spending: Using shopping as a coping mechanism for emotional stress.
4. Accumulating unnecessary debt: Relying on credit cards for everyday expenses without a repayment plan.
5. Lack of budgeting: Not tracking income and expenses, leading to financial disorganization.
6. Overspending on housing: Committing a significant portion of income to housing costs.
7. Neglecting emergency funds: Having no savings for unexpected expenses.
8. Procrastinating on retirement savings: Delaying contributions to retirement accounts.
9. Neglecting insurance coverage: Failing to adequately protect against potential risks.

10. Overreliance on loans: Borrowing excessively for non-essential purchases.

11. Poor investment choices: Making uninformed decisions without proper research.

12. Lack of diversification: Putting all investments in a single asset class, leading to higher risk.

13. Falling for get-rich-quick schemes: Engaging in risky investments promising quick returns.

14. Following herd mentality: Making investment decisions based on others' actions rather than thorough analysis.

15. Neglecting financial education: Failing to continuously learn about personal finance and investing.

16. Ignoring credit scores: Neglecting to monitor and improve credit scores for better financial opportunities.

17. Not negotiating prices: Paying full price without seeking discounts or negotiating better deals.

18. Overspending on lifestyle inflation: Increasing expenses as income rises without saving or investing more.

19. Ignoring tax planning: Failing to optimize tax strategies to minimize liabilities.

20. Relying solely on a single income source: Not diversifying income streams for increased financial security.

21. Gambling or speculative trading: Taking high-risk bets with money instead of making informed investments.

22. Failure to communicate about finances: Avoiding discussions about money within relationships.

23. Not seeking professional financial advice: Failing to consult experts for personalized guidance.

24. Neglecting to track and review financial progress: Not regularly monitoring financial growth or setbacks.

25. Overspending on unnecessary subscriptions and memberships.

26. Neglecting to negotiate higher salaries or better job benefits.

27. Hoarding cash instead of investing it for growth.

28. Neglecting to create a will or establish estate planning.

29. Failing to save for children's education or college expenses.

30. Engaging in retail therapy as a response to stress or emotional distress.

31. Overpaying for convenience instead of seeking cost-saving alternatives.

32. Paying high interest on credit card debt by not paying balances in full.

33. Neglecting to monitor and reduce recurring monthly expenses.

34. Falling for deceptive advertising or marketing tactics.

35. Prioritizing short-term gratification over long-term financial security.

36. Neglecting to negotiate medical expenses and healthcare bills.

37. Lending money to friends or family without proper documentation or repayment plans.

38. Overspending on luxury goods to keep up with social status.

39. Relying on luck or chance for financial success.

40. Overspending on dining out and entertainment.

41. Not reviewing and optimizing investment portfolios regularly.

42. Overspending on unnecessary luxury experiences or vacations.

43. Neglecting to negotiate rent or mortgage terms for better deals.

44. Failing to save for future healthcare expenses and long-term care.

45. Overinvesting in speculative or volatile assets without proper risk assessment.

46. Falling for predatory lending practices and high-interest loans.

47. Not taking advantage of employer-sponsored retirement plans or matching contributions.

48. Relying on payday loans or cash advances with exorbitant interest rates.

49. Overspending on lavish weddings or extravagant celebrations without considering long-term financial implications.

50. Neglecting to update beneficiaries on financial accounts and insurance policies.

"The Art of Self-Compassion in Financial Setbacks"

Financial setbacks are a part of life. Whether it's unexpected expenses, job loss, market downturns, or personal challenges, everyone faces financial storms. It's crucial to acknowledge that setbacks aren't a reflection of your worth or capabilities; they're a natural part of the financial journey. Self-compassion is about treating yourself with the same kindness and understanding you would offer to a friend facing a tough time. When it comes to finances, it's easy to fall into the trap of self-judgment and blame. You might ask yourself, "Why didn't I save more? Why did I make that investment? Why didn't I see this coming?" Instead, self-compassion invites you to reframe those questions with empathy – "What can I learn from this? How can I navigate through this challenge?"

Perfection is an unattainable ideal, especially in the realm of finances. It's okay to make mistakes, encounter setbacks, and face challenges. Self-compassion encourages you to embrace your imperfections, acknowledging that everyone, regardless of appearances, has their share of financial complexities.

The first step towards self-compassion is acknowledging and honoring your feelings. When faced with a financial setback, it's normal to experience a range of emotions – frustration, disappointment, anxiety, or even fear. Instead of suppressing these feelings, give yourself permission to feel them. It's okay not to be okay. Set aside a few moments to reflect on your emotions. Journaling can be a powerful tool to express and process your feelings. Those inner voices might be quick to criticize and blame. Challenge these thoughts by consciously reframing them. If your inner critic says, "I should have known better," counter it with, "I made the best decisions with the information I had at the time." Keep a log of negative thoughts that arise during setbacks. For each one, write a compassionate and realistic response.

When faced with financial setbacks, practicing mindfulness can help you navigate through the challenges without getting entangled in self-blame. Mindfulness allows you to observe your thoughts and emotions without being overwhelmed by them.

It's okay to lean on others for support during challenging times. Share your feelings and experiences with a trusted friend, family member, or financial advisor. Often, an external perspective can provide valuable insights and alleviate feelings of isolation.

Understand that financial setbacks are a part of life, and perfection is an unrealistic standard. Rather than getting stuck in self-blame, channel your energy into creating a plan of action. Break down the steps you need to take to overcome the setback.

The way you treat yourself reflects in your interactions with others. When you practice self-compassion, you're likely to extend that compassion to those around you. Treat yourself with the same kindness you would offer a friend, especially when the seas get rough.

"Rethinking the American Dream"

The traditional image of the American Dream often involves a spacious house with a picket fence. However, rising housing costs and the desire for increased financial freedom are driving individuals to explore alternative housing options.

Tiny houses – where square footage goes on a diet and minimalist living becomes an extreme sport. It's like solving a Rubik's Cube but with your furniture. Suddenly, your cozy little abode is the ultimate multitasker – kitchen by day, bedroom by night, and living room if you're feeling wild. Consider hosting a farewell party for each item you decide to part with. Play "Don't You Forget About Me" by Simple Minds as you lovingly place it in the donation box. Bonus points if you give a heartfelt speech.

Co-living – where sharing is caring, and personal space becomes a flexible concept. It's like having roommates on steroids, minus the passive-aggressive notes about unwashed dishes.

House hacking – turning your home into a money-making wizard by renting out every nook and cranny. It's like Monopoly, but instead of passing "Go" and collecting $200, you're passing your spare room and collecting rent.

RV living – because who needs a fixed address when your home has wheels? It's like a never-ending road trip.

"The Power of Sustainable and Frugal Living"

Ever thought about the magic of turning off lights when you leave a room? It's like a little flick of a wand that reduces your energy consumption and, consequently, your utility bills. Switching to energy-efficient light bulbs, like LED or CFL, might seem like a small change, but it can significantly reduce your energy consumption. Not only do these bulbs last longer, but they also use less electricity, putting a little extra cash in your pocket while reducing your carbon footprint. While on the subject, have you ever thought about upgrading your appliances to more energy-efficient models? Appliances like refrigerators, washing machines, and dishwashers now come with energy-saving features that not only save you money in the long run but also decrease your overall energy consumption. Plus, who wouldn't want to contribute to a greener planet while enjoying the convenience of modern appliances?

Unplug chargers, electronics, and appliances when you're not using them. Even when turned off, these devices often consume standby power. By making a habit of unplugging, you not only save on your energy bill but also help conserve energy on a larger scale.

Here's a small list of sustainable and frugal living practices:

Category	Sustainable and Frugal Living Practices
Energy Efficiency	
Lighting	Switch to LED or CFL bulbs for longer lifespan and lower energy use.
Appliances	Invest in energy-efficient appliances with the ENERGY STAR label.
Unplug and Power	Unplug chargers and electronics when not in

Category	Sustainable and Frugal Living Practices
Down	use to save standby power.
Smart Thermostats	Use a smart thermostat to optimize heating and cooling energy usage.
Waste Reduction	
Reduce, Reuse, Recycle	Choose products with minimal packaging and practice the three Rs.
Composting	Turn kitchen scraps into compost for nutrient-rich soil.
Say No to Single-Use Plastics	Avoid plastic straws, bags, and containers by using reusable alternatives.
Mindful Shopping	Before purchasing, ask if it's a necessity to reduce unnecessary items.
Water Conservation	

Category	Sustainable and Frugal Living Practices
Low-Flow Fixtures	Install low-flow faucets, showerheads, and toilets to reduce water usage.
Rainwater Harvesting	Collect rainwater for watering plants and gardens.
Fix Leaks	Repair any leaks promptly to conserve water and save on water bills.
Gardening and Landscaping	
Native Plants	Opt for native plants in your garden, requiring less water and maintenance.
Mulching	Use mulch to retain soil moisture, suppress weeds, and regulate temperature.
DIY Compost Bin	Create a compost bin for kitchen and garden waste instead of buying one.
Clothing and	

Category	Sustainable and Frugal Living Practices
Textiles	
Second-Hand Shopping	Buy clothing and textiles from thrift stores or online second-hand platforms.
Clothing Swaps	Organize clothing swaps with friends to refresh your wardrobe without spending.
DIY Repairs	Repair clothing items instead of discarding them.
Home Maintenance	
Energy Audits	Conduct home energy audits to identify areas for efficiency improvement.
Insulation Upgrades	Improve home insulation to reduce heating and cooling costs.
DIY Repairs and Maintenance	Learn basic home repair skills to handle minor fixes independently.

Category	Sustainable and Frugal Living Practices
Financial Management	
Cashback and Rewards	Use cashback and rewards programs for credit cards to get discounts on purchases.
Transportation	
Carpooling	Share rides with others to reduce fuel costs and environmental impact.
Bike Commuting	Consider biking to work or for short errands to save on transportation costs.
Public Transportation	Use public transportation for a more cost-effective and eco-friendly commute.

"I love you, but before we say "I Do" let's discuss divorce"

Divorce is an emotionally challenging process that often brings with it complex financial implications. Unfortunately, many individuals find themselves learning crucial lessons about finances in divorce too late—lessons that could have mitigated stress, preserved assets, and paved the way for a more stable post-divorce future.

Many individuals enter marriage with a focus on love and companionship, often neglecting the importance of financial literacy. In divorce, a lack of understanding about shared assets, debts, and financial intricacies can lead to costly mistakes.

Couples fail to have a comprehensive understanding of their shared finances during the marriage. This lack of awareness can lead to disputes during the almost inevitable divorce proceedings, as one or both partners may not have a clear picture of assets, debts, and financial obligations. Failure to document and keep records of financial assets can complicate the property division process. Undervalued or hidden assets may emerge, leading to disputes and potential financial losses for one or both parties.

Many individuals underestimate the importance of having an emergency fund in preparation for the financial changes that come with divorce. Also, delaying legal consultation until the divorce is imminent may lead to inadequate understanding of legal rights and financial entitlements.

Understanding the distinction between equitable distribution and equal division is crucial. While some jurisdictions follow the principle of equal division, others adopt equitable distribution, which considers factors like earning capacity, contributions to the marriage, and future needs.

Valuing assets such as real estate, businesses, and investments can be complex. Individuals often learn too late about the importance of obtaining accurate valuations, as an undervaluation can lead to inequitable asset distribution. Now let's look at Alimony.

Alimony or spousal support is a critical aspect of many divorces, yet individuals often underestimate its significance. Understanding the purpose, types, and tax implications of alimony can profoundly impact financial planning during and after divorce. Lessons are often learned too late regarding the potential modification of alimony. Changes in income, employment, or health can necessitate adjustments, and individuals need to be proactive in addressing such changes through legal channels.

In child custody and support arrangements, the best interests of the child should be paramount. Individuals learn, sometimes belatedly, that financial decisions should align with the child's needs and well-being. Jurisdictions often have guidelines for calculating child support based on factors such as income, custody arrangements, and child-related expenses. Individuals may learn too late about the importance of understanding and complying with these guidelines.

Individuals frequently discover too late the potential consequences of joint debts. Even if the divorce decree assigns responsibility for certain debts, creditors may still hold both parties responsible, impacting credit scores and financial stability. Safeguarding credit is a lesson often learned in hindsight. Establishing individual credit accounts, monitoring credit reports, and addressing joint debts promptly are crucial steps to protect financial well-being post-divorce.

Are there tax implications in divorce? Of course!

Changes in marital status bring about alterations in tax filing status. Individuals may learn too late about the implications of filing as single, head of household, or another status, impacting tax obligations and potential refunds.

While we are on the topic, you might want to fill out a QDRO if you own a retirement account. A QDRO is your Qualified Domestic Relations Order. Individuals with retirement accounts often realize too late the necessity of a Qualified Domestic Relations Order to divide retirement assets. Failure to execute a

QDRO can result in tax penalties and complications in accessing funds.

Post-divorce, individuals may learn the hard way about the importance of updating estate planning documents. Failure to revise wills and beneficiary designations can lead to unintended bequests and inheritance issues.

In the aftermath of divorce, individuals often emerge with a newfound understanding of the intricate relationship between love and money. The lessons learned—ranging from the importance of financial literacy to the complexities of property division, alimony, and estate planning—emphasizes the need for serious financial planning throughout the divorce process.

"Wealth beyond dollars and cents"

Let's start by rewiring our thinking. Wealth isn't merely about the number of zeros in your bank account; it's about abundance in all aspects of life. True wealth is a blend of financial stability, personal growth, vibrant health, and nurturing relationships. It's about embracing a life where every area contributes to a sense of fulfillment. It's also about building resilience and adaptability.

Consider emotional wealth as part of your riches. The trust, love, and understanding within your relationships contribute immeasurably to your overall well-being. These emotional investments pay dividends that financial wealth can't match. Also, your health is perhaps the most precious wealth you possess. Cultivate habits that nourish your body – exercise, a balanced diet, and adequate sleep. A healthy body is a foundation for a fulfilling life.

While financial legacies are common, consider the legacy of positive influence and impact you leave on others. The lives you touch, the inspiration you provide, and the positive change you bring – these are dimensions of wealth that far surpass monetary figures. In cultivating a wealth mindset, don't lose sight of the present. Enjoying the journey, appreciating the small joys, and being fully present in the moment contribute significantly to your wealth in real-time.

Gratitude is the secret sauce that multiplies your wealth. Take a moment each day to acknowledge and appreciate the richness in your life. Gratitude enhances your perspective, fostering a sense of abundance even in the smallest of things. A wealth mindset fueled by gratitude acts as a magnet for positivity. The more you appreciate, the more you attract. It's a powerful cycle that propels you towards a life rich in experiences, relationships, and personal fulfillment. In the pursuit of a wealth mindset, challenges aren't roadblocks but opportunities for growth. Embrace adversity as a chance to learn, evolve, and emerge stronger. The resilience you gain becomes a form of wealth that fortifies your character.

More Books from the Author

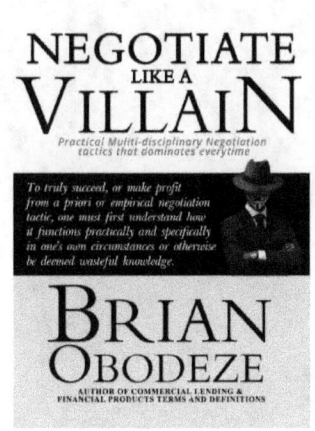

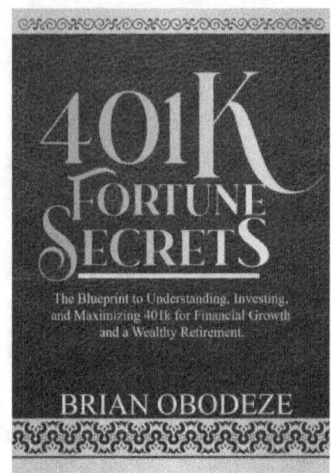

Available on Amazon KDP

www.ingramcontent.com/pod-product-compliance
Lightning Source LLC
Chambersburg PA
CBHW062340290526
45794CB00005B/2069